27 Characters of the Old Testament,

Stories & Activities for Children

Genesis through Daniel

27 Characters of the Old Testament,

Stories & Activities for Children

Genesis through Daniel

By: Jean Ann Williams

Illustrated By: Carley Herlihy

Copyright © 2023: Jean Ann Williams

ISBN: 979-8-9868475-0-4

Illustrated by: Carley Herlihy

Book Designer: Carley Herlihy

First Editor: Barbara Oden

Second Editor: Paula Peckham

Unless otherwise noted, Scriptures are taken from THE HOLY BIBLE, ENGLISH STANDARD VERSION (ESV); Copyright © 2001 by Crossway, a publishing ministry of Good News Publishers. Used by permission.

Use of THE GENEVA BIBLE 1560 EDITION, the words are in **bold** within the text.

Reading Ease: Grade 1 and younger

Dedication

To the children who have been rescued from human trafficking:
It is my prayer each little one will learn about our
Father in Heaven and the real-life characters
written about in God's Holy Word.
People around the world are praying for you!

Note to parents:

The story of Adam is based on fact. But I took the liberty to imagine how Adam might have went about naming a few of the creatures in this story. All the other Biblical accounts had enough information to easily show children how God used people to carry out His plans.

Creative Being ~ Genesis 2:7, 8, 15-20

Riddle: God made me alive. I used my mind to do a job for God. Who am I?

My Story: God formed me of dust from the ground.
He breathed into my nose the breath of life. I was a living soul.
God planted a garden. He put me in it to take care of the garden.
Lord God made every beast out of the ground. He made every bird of the heavens.
He brought them to me. He wanted me to name them.
One flying thing had wings of many colors. I named it dragonfly.
A large beast had four long legs.
Below its round belly hung a soft bag with four tubes. I pressed one. White fluid ran out.
It tasted good and warm. I named this beast cow.

Creative Being ~ Genesis 2:7, 8, 15-20

Bonus: Name God's garden.

A furry animal rubbed my leg. It meowed. I aimed the cow's soft tube
and pressed. The liquid I called milk hit the animal's mouth.
Its tongue licked the milk. I named the furry animal cat.
A bird walked by me. It had long colorful feathers.
The tips of the feathers were shiny.
They looked like eyes. I sighed at its beauty. I named it peacock.
God created them all. I was a creative being. I named them well.

Creative Being Clues

Across

3. Another name for bird. (4)
4. Who am I? (4)
5. Name God's garden. (4)

Down

1. Another word for cat. (6)
2. Female name for the peacock. (6)

9

Obedient Builder ~ Genesis 6:5-22; 7:1-24; 8:6

Riddle: I walked with God. So he gave me a job to save lives. Who am I?

My Story: The Lord was sorry he made man.
His heart was sad. But I made God glad.
God said he was going to destroy the earth. People were sinful. But he wanted to save my family and me. He told me to make an ark. An ark is a boat made of wood. I was to make three levels of rooms in the ark.
God told me to cover the ark with pitch. Inside and out.
This way the ark stayed dry.
My sons and I built the ark like God said. We cut a hole for one window.
We cut a hole for one door.

Obedient Builder ~ Genesis 6:5-22; 7:1-24; 8:6

Bonus: Name how many days the flood rains came down.

God told us to bring creatures into the ark. Beasts, birds, insects, and snakes came. They went into the rooms and nests we made for them. More and more creatures came. We put food in the ark for them to eat. We took food for my family and me.

I was old when we came into the ark. God shut the door. It rained for many days. The flood waters covered the tall hills. The waters stayed on the earth for one hundred fifty days.

God blessed me for being an obedient builder. My family and I lived.

Obedient Builder Clues

Across

2. Another word for animals. (9)
5. Who am I? (4)
6. The flood waters covered the tall _____. (5)

Down

1. I used pitch to keep out _____. (5)
3. My _____ helped me to build the ark. (4)
4. Another word for happy. (4)

Respect of God ~ Genesis 18:1-14; 21:1-8; 22:1-18

Riddle: I showed respect to God. He gave me a living promise. Who am I?

My Story: I rested outside my tent. The Lord came as three men. I
jumped up to meet them. I bowed on the ground. I said I will feed them.
They said for me to do as I have said.
I ran to my wife. I said for her to make cakes. I got a young cow.
I had it cooked. I took milk and the food and set it under the tree.
I watched them eat. They asked where my wife was.
I said she was in the tent. The Lord said he will come in a year.
When he comes back my wife will have a son.

Bonus: Name my wife.

My wife hid at the tent door. She laughed.
She was too old to have a child. The Lord knew my wife had laughed.
He said to me, "Is anything too hard for him?"
I knew the Lord could do anything.
My wife gave birth to a son as the Lord said.
I named him Isaac. "I am filled with laughter for our son," my wife said.
The Lord said he wanted to take Isaac back. I loved my son.
But I did not go against God's word.
God saw my respect of him. He said I may keep Isaac.

Respect of God Clues

Across

2. God told me I may keep _____. (5)
4. My wife was filled with _____ when our son was born. (8)

Down

1. Name my wife. (5)
3. My wife made what kind of food? (4)
5. Who am I? (7)
6. Where was my wife? (4)

Helpful ~ Genesis 24:10-67

Riddle: I was a young woman who helped a man. The man changed my life. Who am I?

My Story: It was time to draw water from the spring.
I enjoyed the fun time at the spring. I visited with my friends.
I walked closer to the spring. A man ran to meet me.
He pointed. "Please give me a little water to drink from your jar."
I gave water to him and his camels. He gave me a ring.
He gave me two bracelets for my arms. I told him my name.
I invited him to spend the night at my mother's home.
The man bowed his head. He worshipped the Lord.
"Blessed be the Lord. He is the God of my master."

Helpful ~ Genesis 24:10-67

Bonus: Name the master and his son.

I ran home and told my family what happened.
The man soon came to my house. He told me God chose me to marry his master's son.
The man said I was to leave with him the next day. My family asked me if I wanted to go.
I said yes. I believed the man. So, I left with him when the sun rose.
We came at the place where I would live.
A man came to meet us on the road. This man was the master's son.
I became his wife. I was helpful. God blessed me.
My husband loved me with all his heart.

Helpful Clues

Across

5. Who am I? (7)
6. I gave water to his _____. (6)

Down

1. What did the man give to me for my arms? (9)
2. Name the master. (7)
3. My husband loved me with all his _____. (5)
4. Name the son. (5)

21

Riddle: I was a cheat. Someone wanted revenge. Who am I?

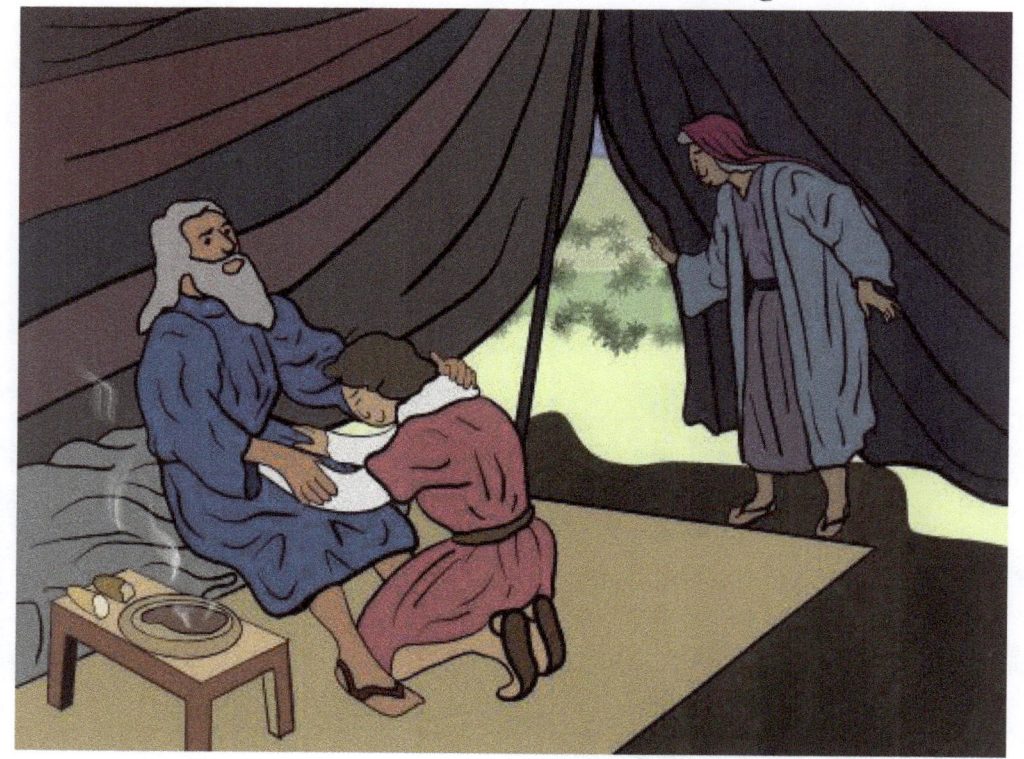

My Story: I fooled Father into blessing me.
My twin should have been the one blessed. My twin was angry.
Our father sent me away. Years went by. I sent my men to talk to my twin.
To see if he still hated me. My men told me my twin was coming.
He had 400 of his men. I was scared. I prayed for the Lord to save me.
My twin may still want to hurt me. I told my men to take some of my stock.
Give them as gifts to my twin. A man wrestled with me in the night time. He hit my hip.
It hurt. He told me to let him go. But I said he had to bless me.

Perseverance ~ Genesis
27:41; 28:5; 31:38; 32:1-21, 24-31; 33:1-11
Bonus: Name my twin.

The man said I had a new name.
He called me Israel. I had acted in perseverance. I had not backed down.
So he blessed me. And I had seen God face to face.
But I had a limp from where he hurt my hip.
Soon my twin ran to me. He hugged me. He kissed me. We wept.
He took my presents to show his love.
God blessed me again. My twin and I were friends.

Perseverance Clues

Across

3. I made my _____ angry with my trick. (7)
5. Who did I fool? (6)

Down

1. Who am I? (5)
2. I saw _____ face to face. (3)
4. Name my twin. (4)
6. A man wrestled with me and hurt my _____. (3)

Merciful Brother ~ Genesis
37:3-13, 18-28; 39:1-5; 42:5-10; 43:1, 2; 45:1-5, 28

Riddle: I was once a slave. I was merciful to my brothers. Who am I?

My Story: I was a boy. My brothers talked mean to me.
I told them about my dreams. That they would bow before me.
Their hate grew. My oldest brother gave an order.
"Shed no blood. Put him into this pit. But do not lay a hand on him." He left.
My other brothers did not kill me. They sold me. I became a slave.
The Lord was with me as I grew up. I had good jobs.
Now my job was to sell grain to the people.
One day my brothers came to me to buy grain. They did not know me.
And they bowed before me.

Merciful Brother ~ Genesis
37:3-13, 18-28; 39:1-5; 42:5-10; 43:1, 2; 45:1-5, 28
Bonus: Name the land that had the grain.

But I acted like they were not my brothers.
And they came to me once again. My heart moved with joy to see them.
I now wanted my brothers to know who I was.
I began to cry. They had looks of fear. I calmed myself.
I said to them that I was their brother. The one they sold as a slave.
But I did not want them to feel sad. God had wanted me here.
I helped to feed the people. I was merciful to my brothers. God blessed me.
We were a family again.

Merciful Brother Clues

Across

1. I was merciful to whom? (8)
2. Who am I? (6)
3. Name the land that had the grain. (5)

Down

1. My brothers _____ before me. (5)
2. My heart moved with _____ to see my brothers. (3)
4. I sold _____ to the people. (5)

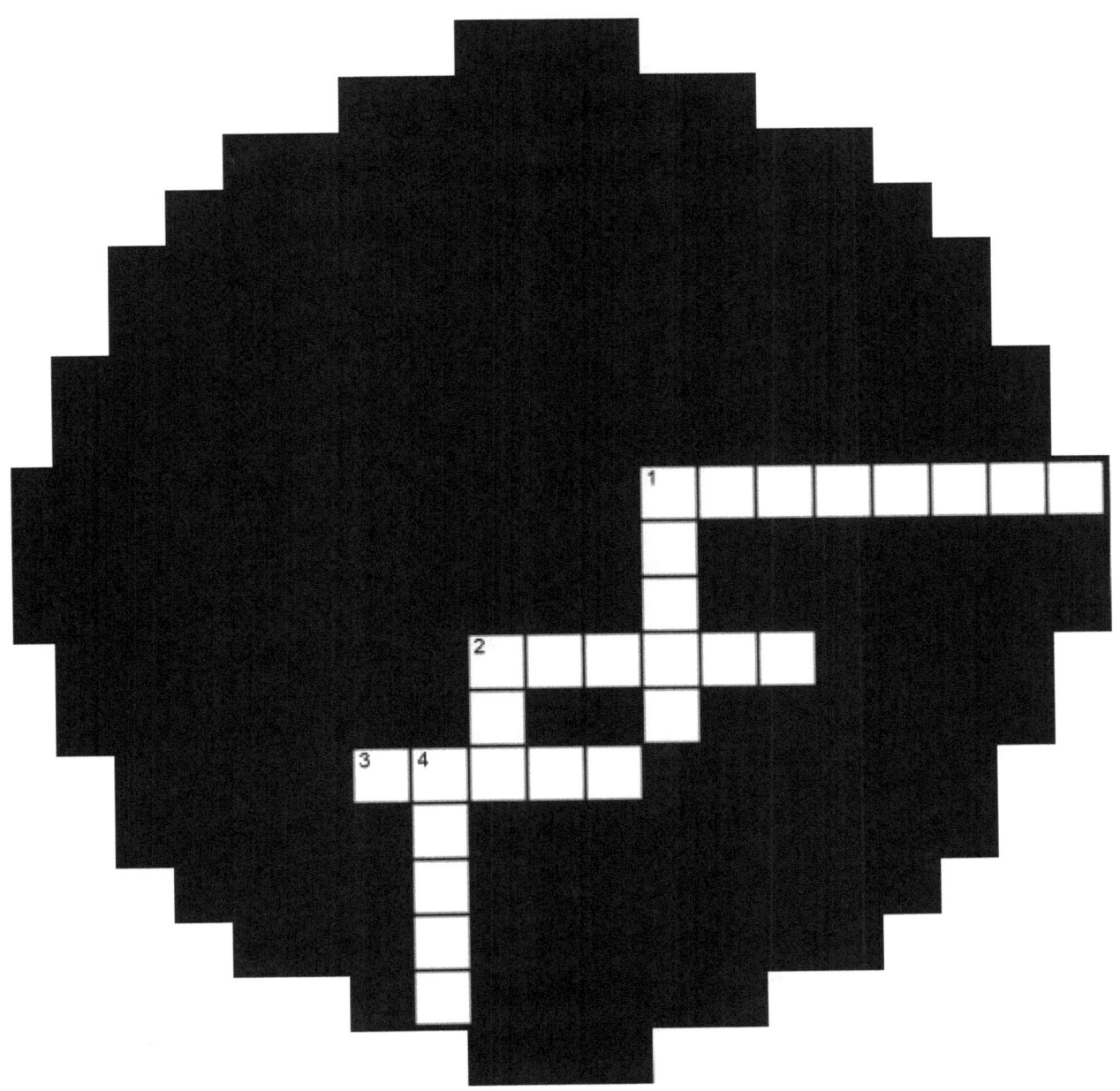

29

Kinship ~ Exodus 1:15-17; 2:1-10; 3:6-10

Riddle: Our family broke the law. I helped to save our baby. Who am I?

My Story: I waited for Mom to have her baby. A baby cried.
He was a fine child. Born a slave. But the mean king killed boy babies.
We hid the baby in our house. But Mom could not hide him for long.
She made a tiny boat. She put pitch on it to keep out the water.
Mom laid the baby inside. She fit a lid on top. She put his boat on the river.
I swam to watch it float. The king's daughter took a bath. She saw the boat. She told her maid to bring it to her. Would she tell the king about the baby? The maid pushed the boat to the king's daughter. She opened the lid. The baby cried.

Bonus: Name my brother.

She scooped the baby up. She hugged him. I drew closer.
I asked if she wanted me to find a mama to feed the baby milk.
The king's daughter said yes. I took Mom to the king's daughter.
She told my mom to keep the baby and feed him.
Mom fed him until he was older. She gave him back to the king's daughter.
I protected my kin. God blessed me and others.
My brother became a man. He took our people to freedom.

Kinship Clues

Across

2. My brother was born a _____. (5)
3. My brother became a man who led our people to _____. (7)
5. Mom gave my brother back to the king's _____. (8)

Down

1. Mom made a tiny _____. (4)
2. Who am I? (6)
4. Name my brother. (5)

Spokespersons ~ Exodus 3:2-15; 4:1-5, 10-17, 27-31; 8:1-6; 12:29-32; 14:21-28; 15:4

Riddle: God gave my brother and me a job. Our people were slaves.

Our Story: God met me at a fiery bush. I was afraid to look at him.
God said he knew his people cried.
He said for me to tell his people that I Am has sent me.
I did not think the people would believe me. God said for me to use my long stick.
Show the people how my long stick can make things.
But now I said I was too slow with my words.
God said my brother was good with his words.
And my brother was to meet with me. I met my brother.
I told him he had to talk to the bad king. To tell him to let God's people go.

Spokespersons ~ Exodus 3:2-15; 4:1-5, 10-17, 27-31; 8:1-6; 12:29-32; 14:21-28; 15:4

Bonus: Name the sea.

Now my brother talked to the king. The king did not let the people go.
My stick made a snake. It made frogs that hopped on the king.
My stick made many bad things. And the king let God's people go.
We ran away to the sea. I put out my hand toward the sea.
This is what God told me to do. The water split in two.
The people walked upon dry land to the other side.
God blessed us as his spokespersons. God did not bless the king.

Spokespersons Clues

Across

1. The sea split in _____. (3)
4. Name the sea. (3)
5. God told me to use my long _____. (5)

Down

2. God said my brother was good with _____. (5)
3. My staff turned into a _____. (5)

Diligence ~ Numbers 22:9-35

Riddle: God gave me a command. I wanted to do it my way. Who am I?

My Story: A king's son wanted me to fight his foes.
He knew my God could make his foes go away. But I had to ask God.
God said for me to not go. These people were blessed. So I did not.
But the king's son told his men to talk to me again. I still said no.
Not even if he gave me money. I did not want to disobey God.
God came to me when the sun went down.
He told me to go if the men asked me again. The sun rose in the sky.
The men did not ask me. But I went with them anyway. God was angry.
I had disobeyed him.

Bonus: Name my animal.

I rode my animal for a while. Soon she went off the road.
I hit my animal to go back. She did. But she stopped. I hit my animal again. But she spoke
like a human. "Have I ever not done what you wanted?"
God opened my eyes. An Angel of God stood with his sword drawn.
I bowed down. My face hit the dirt. I had sinned.
The men had not asked me to go with them.
But now the Angel said for me to go. God forgave me.
I wanted to act in diligence. To obey my Lord and God.

Diligence Clues

Across

4. I did not want to _____ God. (7)
5. Now who said for me to go with the men? (5)

Down

1. I would not fight their foes even if they gave me _____. (5)
2. A king's son wanted me to fight his _____. (4)
3. Who am I? (6)
4. Name my animal. (6)

Duty Bound ~ Joshua 1:1-3; 3:5-8, 14-17; 4:14

Riddle: One day Moses died. I led God's people the rest of the way to a new land. Who am I?

My Story: I told the people to bless themselves.
God would make them feel in awe of me.
The Lord said he will make me good in the eyes of his people.
The same as he did for Moses. I told the people God's plan.
The priests were to carry the ark of God.
They were to walk to a river. They were to stand in the water.
We were to cross the river. God would make our foes leave.
God said the land on the other side was ours. We came to the river.

Duty Bound ~ Joshua 1:1-3; 3:5-8, 14-17; 4:14

Bonus: Name the river.

The priests held the ark of the covenant.
They stood in the low water of the river. We waited.
Then God made the waters flowing down to go up.
The waters went up. Up. Up. And far away.
The priests who carried the ark walked on dry land.
God's people walked on dry land. We made it to the other side of the river.
I had obeyed God. I did my duty to him.
He blessed us as we went to a land he had givin to us.

Duty Bound Clues

Across

1. The people left _____ just like God told them to. (4)
5. The priests held the ark of the _____. (8)
6. Name the river. (6)

Down

2. God would make the people feel in _____ of me. (3)
3. I told the people of God's _____. (4)
4. Who am I? (6)

Kindness ~ Joshua 2:3, 6-21; 6:1-3, 15, 16, 20, 23

Riddle: I was a woman. I hid the strangers. Who am I?

My Story: I hid the strangers on my roof. I did not want the king's men
to find them. I told the kings men the strangers went out the gate.
The king's men ran after them. But the strangers were safe with me.
I knew the Lord gave the strangers and their people our land.
Would they let me and my family live? The strangers said yes.
But I was not to tell anyone. They were to bring back an army.
They would treat me and my family with kindness. Like the kindness I had shown to
them. The strangers told me to hang a red cord in my window. The red cord would show
them it was my house. They would save me and my family.

Kindness ~ Joshua 2:3, 6-21; 6:1-3, 15, 16, 20, 23

Bonus: Name my city.

I lowered the men down from my roof. Days went by.
Soon, I waited no more. The army marched around our city walls for six days.
They blew loud horns. They shouted on day seven.
They marched seven times around the city.
Then the walls fell flat. My family and I went to the red-cord window.
We waited. We looked for the two strangers called spies. Did they forget us?
God blessed my kindness. The spies took me and my family with them.
Then the army took my city.

Kindness Clues

Across

3. The army shouted on day _____. (5)
4. The strangers told me to hang a red _____ in my window. (4)
6. I lowered the strangers down from my _____. (4)

Down

1. I hid strangers who were called _____. (5)
2. Name my city. (7)
5. The spies were to bring back an _____. (4)

Riddle: I was a woman. I judged God's people. Who am I?

My Story: I sat under a tree. People came to me for rulings.
I took time to hear what people had to say. I worked hard to be fair.
I sent for Barak. I told him God wanted him to get his men.
God said Barak was to meet the foes. Barak said he would go.
But only if I went with him. I said yes.
And I told him this fight would not be to his glory.
God would sell our foes into the hands of a woman.
I arose and went with Barak. He got many more men to help in the fight.

Bonus: Name our foe.

Then I said to Barak, "Up!"
This was the day God would give Barak our foes. God went before Barak.
His men fought too. There were no more foes left.
Then we sang. "Praise ye the Lord! He avenged Israel."
And that our people were willing to fight. Bless the Lord!
I was known as a good judge for my fairness. And God blessed us.
He gave me a message for Barak.

Fairness Clues

Across

1. We _____ about our people who were willing to fight. (4)
3. Who am I? (7)
5. God would go before _____. (5)

Down

1. Name our foe. (6)
2. I told Barak this fight would not be to his _____. (5)
4. I took time to _____ what the people had to say. (4)

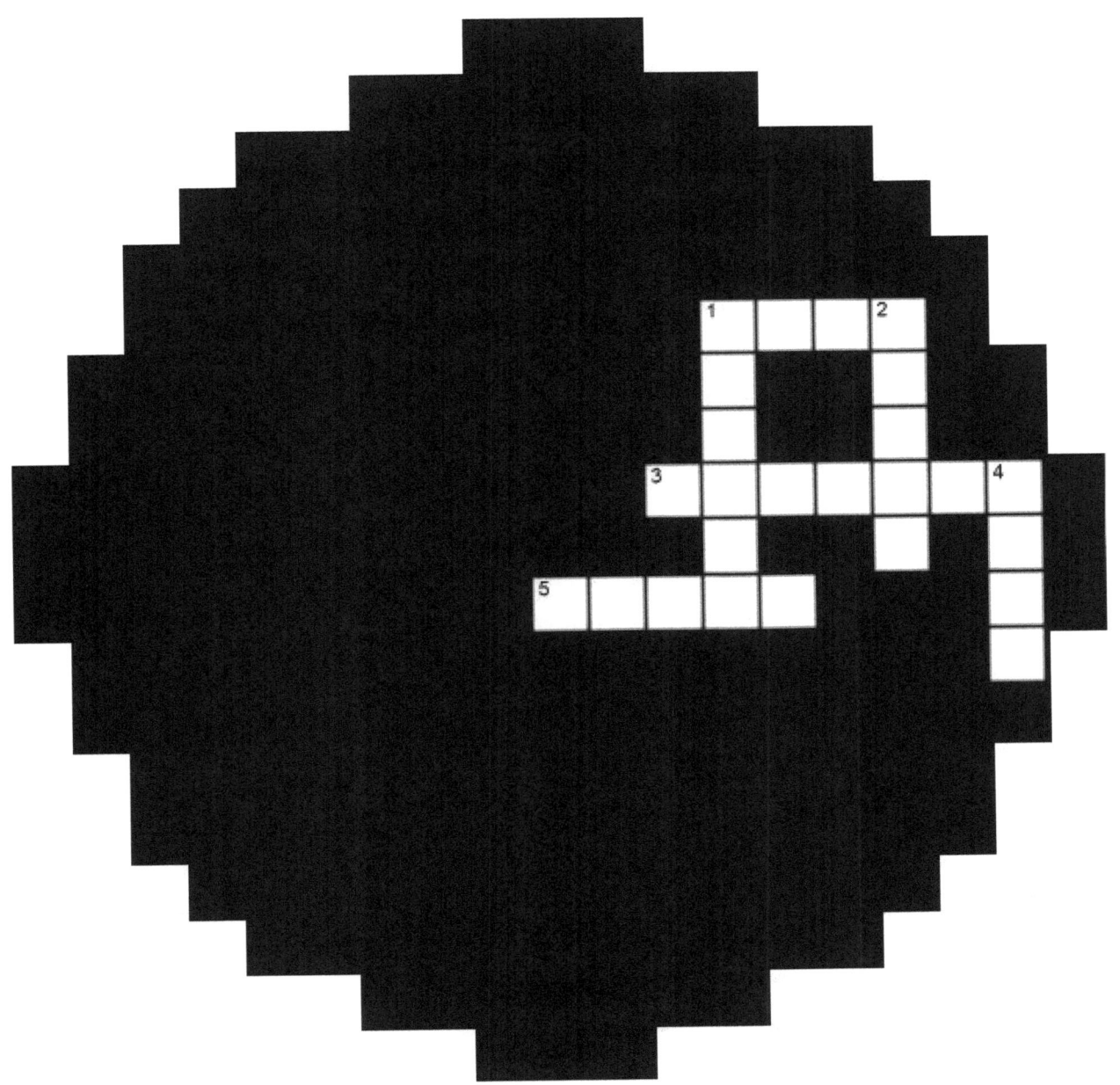

53

Valor ~ Judges 6:11-23, 36-40; 7:2, 8, 16-18, 21

Riddle: Burned food proved who spoke to me. Drops of water told me of my job. Who am I?

My Story: I worked to take grains of wheat from a plant.
Then an angel of the Lord came to me. I stopped my work.
He told me I was a man of valor. The angel told me to save my people from our foes.
But was this really an angel of the Lord?
The angel told me to set meat and bread on a rock. I poured broth over the food.
He poked the broth-soaked meat and bread with a stick.
Fire rose from the rock and burned the food.
I now believed he was an angel of the Lord.

Valor ~ Judges 6:11-23, 36-40; 7:2, 8, 16-18, 21

Bonus: Name the size of our army.

But did the Lord want me to save my people?
I told the Lord I wanted to be sure. I laid a wool fleece on the dirt.
I wanted morning dew to cover only the wool.
The next morning the dirt was dry. I squeezed water from the fleece.
I asked God to please show me one last clue. I wanted the fleece dry.
I wanted the dirt wet. And God did this for me. Now I knew.
The Lord made my army small. We marched. We blew trumpets.
We shouted. "For the Lord and for Gideon." Our foes ran from us.
God blessed me for my valor.

Valor Clues

Across

2. Who am I? (6)
4. The _____ made my army small. (4)
6. I squeezed _____ from the fleece. (5)

Down

1. Who told me to set meat and bread on a rock? (5)
3. What instrument did we blow? (8)
5. The angel said I was a man of _____. (5)

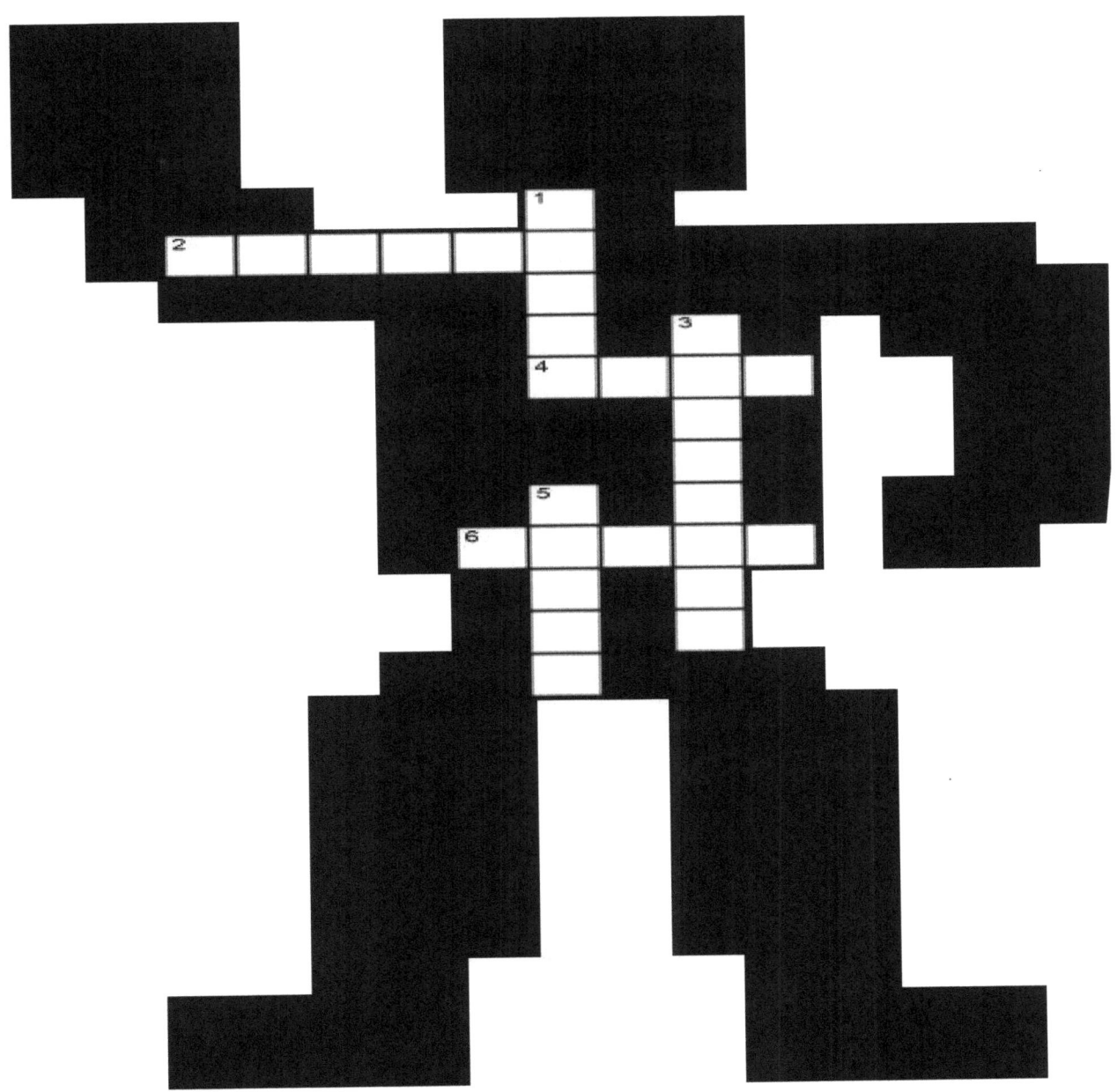

Spirit-filled Man ~ Judges 13:2-5, 24, 25; 14:5-9; 15:4-15, 18-20

Riddle: God gave me a gift. And it was a secret. Who am I?

My Story: An angel told my mom I would be special. Then I was born.
I became a man. One day a lion growled at me. The Spirit of God filled me.
I became strong. I tore the lion up with my bare hands.
Some days passed. I walked to where the dead lion lay.
A swarm of bees and honey were in the body of the lion.
I dug in my hands. I filled them with the honey. I ate some honey.
I gave honey to my mom and dad.

Spirit-filled Man ~ Judges 13:2-5, 24, 25; 14:5-9; 15:4-15, 18-20

Bonus: Name my gift.

One day I made my foes angry. My friends were upset with me too.
They said our foes rule us. I must not make them angry. I did not agree.
But I let my friends tie my hands with rope.
I let them take me to our foes. Our foes wanted to kill me.
The Spirit of God filled me. My ropes melted from my hands.
I picked up a jaw bone. I struck down our foes. I helped our people that day.
God blessed me again. He made me judge of our people.

Spirit-filled Man Clues

Across

2. Name my gift. (6)
4. What growled at me? (4)

Down

1. God blessed me again when he made me a _____ of our people. (5)
2. Who am I? (6)
3. My friends tied my hands with _____. (4)

61

Caring Friend ~ Ruth 1:3-8, 14-18; 2:1-18; 4:7-10, 14-17

Riddle: I was a woman. I took care of my husband's mom. Who am I?

My Story: Our husbands had died. I stayed with her.
My husband's mom heard about free grain. We left our home.
We went to the place of free grain.
I told her to let me go to get the grain left by the pickers.
I said, "The man who owns the field may be kind to me."
I got grain from the field. The man who owned it saw me.
He told me to stay in his field to pick the left-over grains.
I could even drink his water. I said, "Why are you being kind?"

Caring Friend ~ Ruth 1:3-8, 14-18; 2:1-18; 4:7-10, 14-17

Bonus: Name the field owner.

He told me people said I was a caring friend to my husband's mom.
He learned I had stayed with her after our husbands died.
That I came to a land I did not know.
He found out I believed in the one true God. Not the fake gods of my home.
The field owner gave me bread. I ate. I became full. I saved some for my husband's mom.
The owner talked to his young men.
They were to let me take grain from where they had not yet picked.
God blessed me for being a caring friend.
Soon after, I married the field owner. We had a son. He was the grandfather of King David.

Caring Friend Clues

Across

2. Who am I? (4)
3. _____ blessed me for being a caring friend. (3)
5. Name the field owner. (4)

Down

1. The field owner gave me _____ to eat. (5)
3. I got _____ from the field. (5)
4. Name my son who became grandfather to King David. (4)

Dependable ~ 1 Samuel 1:8-17, 20-28; 2:18-21

Riddle: I had no children. But I was a dependable woman. Who am I?

My Story: My husband and I went to tabernacle each year. I cried.
I made a vow in my heart. If only the Lord would give me a son.
I would give him back to the Lord. He would serve the Lord all his life.
Eli the priest saw my lips move as I prayed. He thought I was drunk.
I told him I spoke from grief. Not from too much strong drink.
He said, "May God grant your request." I left the tabernacle.
Eli's words made my husband and me glad.
Soon my belly grew large with a baby.

Bonus: Name the son I gave back.

The baby was a gift from God. And I still had to keep my vow.
I would do so to thank the Lord. Now my son grew and grew on my milk.
One day I took him off of my milk. I took him to the priest.
My son ministered to the Lord with the priest.
My husband and I went to see our son each year.
I sewed a new and bigger robe for him each year.
The priest prayed for the Lord to give my husband and me more children.
I was dependable. So, God gave us three more boys and two girls.
Our first son grew before the Lord.

Dependable Clues

Across

3. I made a _____ in my heart. (3)
5. I was _____. (10)
6. Eli's words made my husband and me _____. (4)

Down

1. Name my son. (6)
2. I sewed a _____ for my son each year. (4)
4. Who am I? (6)

Responsible ~ 1 Samuel 9:15-21, 27; 10:1, 5-10, 20-26

Riddle: I left home to look for lost donkeys. I came back a king. Who am I?

My Story: I needed to find my lost donkeys.
The Prophet Samuel told me not to look for them. They had been found.
He told me God desired me and my father's house for Israel.
I did not understand. My tribe was the least of all the tribes of Israel.
Samuel told me about the Word of God. He poured oil on my head.
He kissed me. He said the Lord anointed me.
The prophet said I would be a prince for God's people.

Bonus: Name my tribe.

The Prophet Samuel said the Spirit of the Lord would come on me.
I would talk like the prophets. I went to a city. A group of people met with me. The Spirit
of God came on me. God gave me a new heart.
I prophesied among the prophets. But I was too scared to be prince.
The people found me and took me from where I hid.
I was much taller than all of the people. They said, "Long live the king!"
I took a band of men to my home. God had also touched their hearts.
I was no longer scared to be king. God blessed me because I was responsible.

Responsible Clues

Across

2. What was lost? (7)
5. My tribe was the _____ of all the tribes of Israel. (5)
6. God gave me a new _____. (5)

Down

1. I was no longer scared to be _____. (4)
3. Who am I? (4)
4. I was much _____ than all of the people. (6)

Peacemaker ~ 1 Samuel 16:1-13

Riddle: God told me to find a new king. But I feared King Saul. Who am I?

My Story: God rejected Saul. God told me to fill my horn with oil.
He said he would send me to a man who had many sons.
"I have given for myself a king among his sons."
I said, "How can I go? Saul will find out and kill me."
God told me to take a cow.
He told me to say, "I have come to cook the cow for the Lord."
I came to the town. The elders met me in fear. I told them I came in peace.
I invited the elders to eat the cow with me. I told the father and his sons to eat.
First, I had the sons of the man pass by me.

Peacemaker ~ 1 Samuel 16:1-13

Bonus: Name the new king.

I asked God if he wanted this son or that one.
God said no to all seven sons. I said to the father, "Are all your sons here?"
The father had one more son. He was the youngest. The boy passed by me.
He had beautiful eyes. He was handsome. The Lord said, "This is he."
I poured oil on the boy. The Spirit of God came on him.
The Spirit stayed with him from that day.
God blessed me as a peacemaker. I found the new king for our people.

Peacemaker Clues

Across

2. The elders met me in _____. (4)
3. The _____ of God came on the boy. (6)
5. God told me to fill my horn with _____. (3)

Down

1. Name the new king. (5)
3. Who am I? (6)
4. I was to cook a _____ for the Lord. (3)

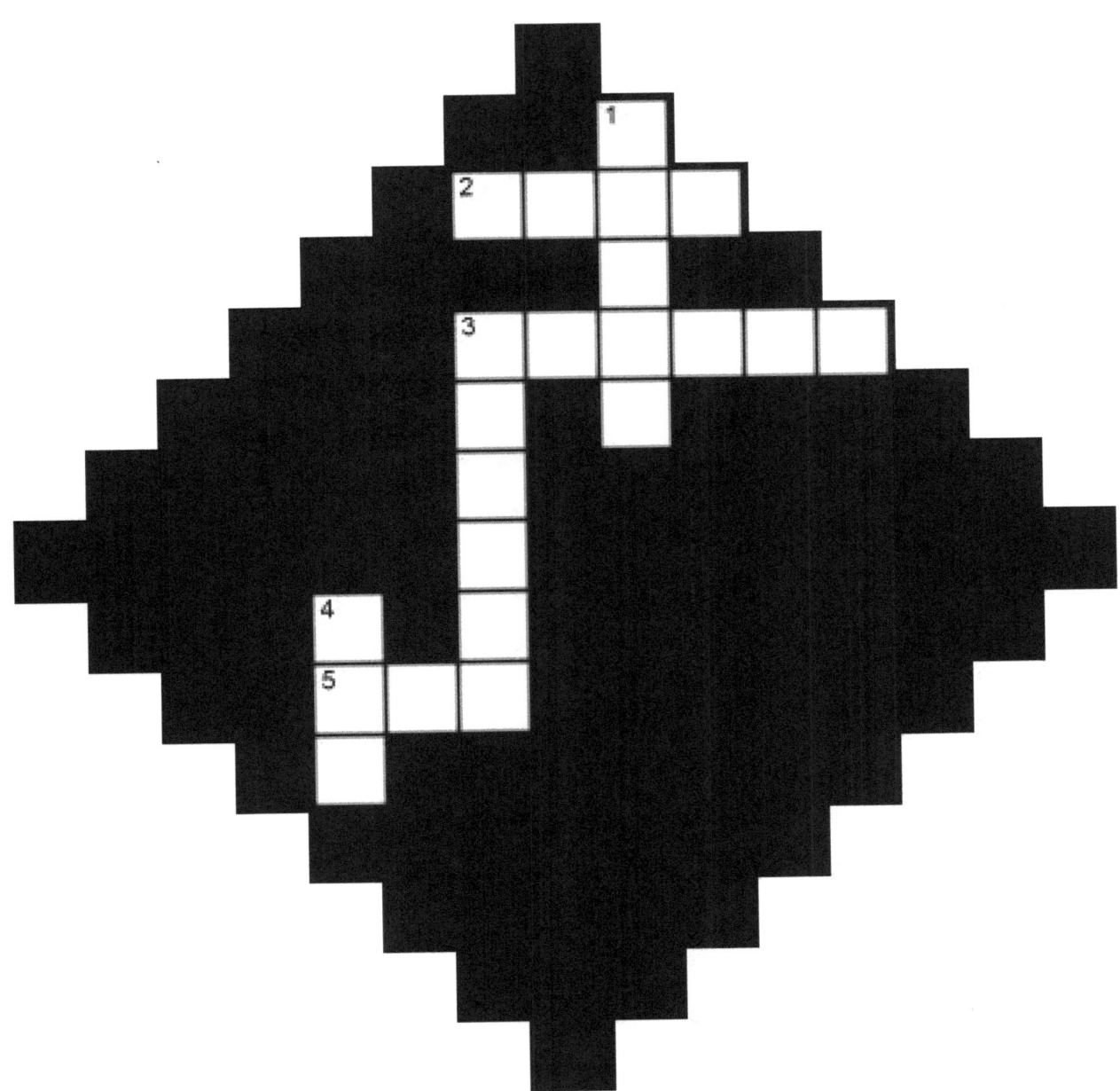

Courage ~ 1 Samuel 17:3, 4, 10, 11, 20-23, 32-37, 40-50

Riddle: I was a boy. I was not afraid. Who am I?

My Story: A giant man shouted at our men.
He wanted our men to choose one man.
The giant wanted that man to come down to him. I stood before the king.
I said I wanted to fight the giant. The Lord saved me from the paw of the lion. He saved
me from the paw of the bear.
I knew he would save me from this giant.
The king said, "The Lord be with you."
I gathered five rocks at a stream. I got closer to the giant. He was huge.
The giant said, "Am I a dog? That you come at me with sticks?"

Courage ~ 1 Samuel 17:3, 4, 10, 11, 20-23, 32-37, 40-50

Bonus: Name the giant.

I spoke to the giant. "You come to me with a sword.
And you have a spear. But I come to you in the name of the Lord.
For this is the battle of the Lord. He will give you over to me and our army."
I reached into my shepherd bag. I placed a rock on the leather of my slingshot. I pulled
back. Aimed. Fired. The rock struck the giant in the forehead.
The giant fell facedown. I won the battle for my people.
God was indeed with me.

Courage Clues

Across

1. I reached into my shepherd's _____. (3)
4. I said I wanted to fight the _____. (5)
5. I gathered _____ rocks at a brook. (4)

Down

1. I won the _____ for my people. (6)
2. Name the giant. (7)
3. Who am I? (5)

Loyal ~ 1 Samuel 24:1-12, 17-23; 26:1-18, 21-25; 31:6; 2 Samuel 5:3, 4

Riddle: I was loyal to King Saul. But he wanted me gone. Who am I?

My Story: King Saul was told that I wanted to harm him.
My men and I hid from the king in a cave.
One day, the king came in our cave. I crawled to where he was.
I cut off a tip of his robe. King Saul left the cave. I stood a short distance from him.
I bowed. I said, "See the tip of your robe in my hand?" I did not want to kill the king.
And I had not sinned against him. Yet he hunted me.
King Saul did not want to be mean to me. So now he cried.
But then the king changed his mind. I still had to hide.

Loyal ~ 1 Samuel 24:1-12, 17-23; 26:1-18, 21-25; 31:6; 2 Samuel 5:3, 4

Bonus: Name my age as the new king.

One night, I crept into King Saul's camp.
The Lord put the king and his army in a deep sleep. I did not want to kill God's anointed.
Instead, I took the king's sword and water jug. These things lay by his head.
I climbed a hill. I shouted at the man who was to protect the king.
But he did not on this night. Again I did not harm the king.
So I returned the sword to the king. The king rewarded my loyalty. He went on his way.
I went on my way. The king died. I no longer lived in caves.
God blessed me for being loyal. I became the new king of Israel.

Loyal Clues

Across

2. Who am I? (5)
5. The Lord put the king and his army in a deep _____. (5)

Down

1. Where did my men and I hide? (4)
3. I became the new king of _____. (6)
4. The king did not want to be _____ to me. (4)

Wisdom ~ 1 Kings 3:5-14; 4:29-34; 10:1-10

Riddle: My dad, the king, had died. Now I became the king. Who am I?

My Story: I followed the law as did my dad. And I asked God for wisdom.
He gave me more. The years went by. One day, a queen came to meet me.
She had heard of my fame. She came to test me with hard questions.
The queen told me what was on her mind. I told her all she wanted to know. She saw the
wisdom God gave to me.
Now the queen had no more questions. She looked at all I had.
She had not believed the reports about me. The queen saw with her own eyes. It was all
true.

Wisdom ~ 1 Kings 3:5-14; 4:29-34; 10:1-10

Bonus: Name the queen's country.

The queen said, "Your men are happy!
Your servants are happy to hear your wisdom."
She said, "Blessed be the Lord your God who loves you.
So, he made you king." She saw that I was a fair and good king.
The queen gave me many gifts. She gave me gold.
She gave me a large amount of spices and precious stones.
No one after that gave me such large amounts of spices. God blessed me.
I was wiser than all men. I spoke proverbs. I made songs.
God blessed others. They read my proverbs and songs.

Wisdom Clues

Across

3. Who am I? (7)
4. The queen gave me many _____. (5)
5. The queen came to test me with hard _____. (9)

Down

1. The queen saw the _____ God gave to me. (6)
2. I made _____. (5)
3. Name the queen's country. (5)

Man of God ~ 2 Kings 1:2-17

Riddle: I was a prophet of God. I spoke for God. Who am I?

My Story: An angel of the Lord spoke to me.
He said I was to meet with the men of a king. That king lay sick in his bed. The king had sent his men to speak to a fake god.
The king wanted to know if he would die.
I told the men the king would die. The men told the king.
The king did not like my words. He sent a captain and his men to me.
The captain found me on a hill. He gave me a message from the king.
"Oh, man of God, the king says, 'Come down.'"

Man of God ~ 2 Kings 1:2-17

Bonus: Name the country of the king..

I looked at the captain. "If I am a man of God, let fire come down from heaven.
It will destroy you and your men." Then the fire did so.
The king sent to me a second captain with his men. I told the fire to destroy them.
It did so. The king sent a third captain with many more men.
This captain begged for his life.
The angel of the Lord told me to go with the captain. I met with the king.
I told him what God had wanted. God expected the king to come to him.
Not go to a fake god about his future. Now the king would die.
I obeyed the Lord as a man of God.

Man of God Clues

Across

2. Name the country of the king. (7)
4. This captain _____ for his life. (6)
6. Who am I? (6)

Down

1. Let fire come down from _____. (6)
3. Who spoke to me? (5)
5. The king sent to me a third _____. (7)

Tenacity ~ 2 Kings 2:1-11

Riddle: The Lord was about to take my friend up to heaven. Who am I?

My Story: My friend and I were walking.
He said for me to stay at a town while he walked on. I told him no.
People met us at the next town.
They told me the Lord was going to take my friend. I said, "Yes I know."
And I told them to keep quiet. Again, my friend told me to stay in that town. The Lord was
to send him to a city. I said no.
I did not want to leave my friend. We came to a river. My friend rolled his coat. He hit the
water with his coat. The river parted.
We walked on dry ground to the other side.

Bonus: Name my friend.

My friend was about to be taken from me.
He said, "What do you want before I leave you?"
I asked my friend to give me double the amount of his spirit.
He said I asked a hard thing.
He said I could have a double amount of his spirit.
But only if I were to see him being taken.
Then chariots and horses of fire came between us.
My friend went up into heaven by a whirlwind. I pleased God.
I had tenacity to not leave my friend. And God gave me the spirit of my friend.

Tenacity Clues

Across

4. Name my friend. (6)
5. My friend went into heaven in a _____. (9)
6. Who am I? (6)

Down

1. I did not want to leave my _____. (6)
2. My friend rolled his _____ and hit the water. (4)
3. I asked my friend to give me double the amount of his _____. (6)

Cooperation ~ Esther 2:15, 17; 3:8, 9, 13; 4:1, 3-14; 6:14; 7:1-6, 10

Riddle: I was a queen. My people were in danger. Who am I?

My Story: A bad man said my kin had wrong laws.
He said our laws did not keep the law of the king.
This bad man made the king believe this lie. Now my kin had to be killed.
The bad man sent letters to all the lands of the king.
The letters said to kill all my kin in one day. I had a cousin who raised me.
He tore his clothes in grief. He put ashes on himself. He cried.
My kin also heard the news. They no longer ate. They cried.
I was told what the bad man had done. I, too, was sad.

Bonus: Name my cousin.

My cousin asked me to beg the king to help our kin. I was scared.
No one goes to the king without being invited. The king must ask to see a person.
Even to see me, his queen.
My cousin told me I would die, too, if all our people were killed.
It would not matter that I was queen. He said, "You may be queen for such a time as this."
I went to the king. I fed him a meal. He was happy.
I then asked him to stop the bad man and his plan. The king said my kin will live.
God blessed me. He chose me to help in cooperation to save my kin.

Cooperation Clues

Across

3. Name my cousin. (8)
4. My cousin asked me to _____ the king to help our kin. (3)
6. My cousin said, "You may be queen for such a _____ as this. (4)

Down

1. My cousin put _____ on himself. (5)
2. A bad man said my kin had laws that were _____. (5)
5. Who am I? (6)

Integrity ~ Job 1:7-22; 2:3-13; 3:1; 13:15; 27:5, 6; 42:10-16

Riddle: God gave me much. Satan stole it all. Who am I?

My Story: The Lord told Satan, "Behold, all that he has is in your hand.
Only do not kill him." So, Satan left the presence of the Lord.
He began to test me. Men gave me bad news. Foes took my animals.
The fire of God came from the heaven and burned my sheep.
A wind blew the house upon my children. I arose and tore my robe.
I shaved my head. I fell on the ground to worship God. I knew the Lord gave.
I knew he took away. Blessed be the name of the Lord.
I did not sin in all this. I did not blame God for my losses.

Integrity ~ Job 1:7-22; 2:3-13; 3:1; 13:15; 27:5, 6; 42:10-16

Bonus: Name my first daughter.

Satan tested me once again. My body broke out in sores.
My friends came to visit. They did not recognize me.
My sores were bad. So, my friends cried. They tore their robes in grief.
They put dust on their heads. They sat with me for seven days.
We did not speak. I was in such agony. I was sorry that I was ever born.
Though God slay me, I will hope in him. I will trust in him.
My kin comforted me because of my losses. They gave me a piece of silver and a gold ring.
God blessed my integrity. He gave me more than before. My wife had ten more children.

Integrity Clues

Across

3. Name my first daughter. (7)
5. I arose and _____ my robe. (4)

Down

1. I fell on the ground to _____ God. (7)
2. I did not _____ God for my losses. (5)
3. Who am I? (3)
4. Though God slay me, I will _____ in him. (4)

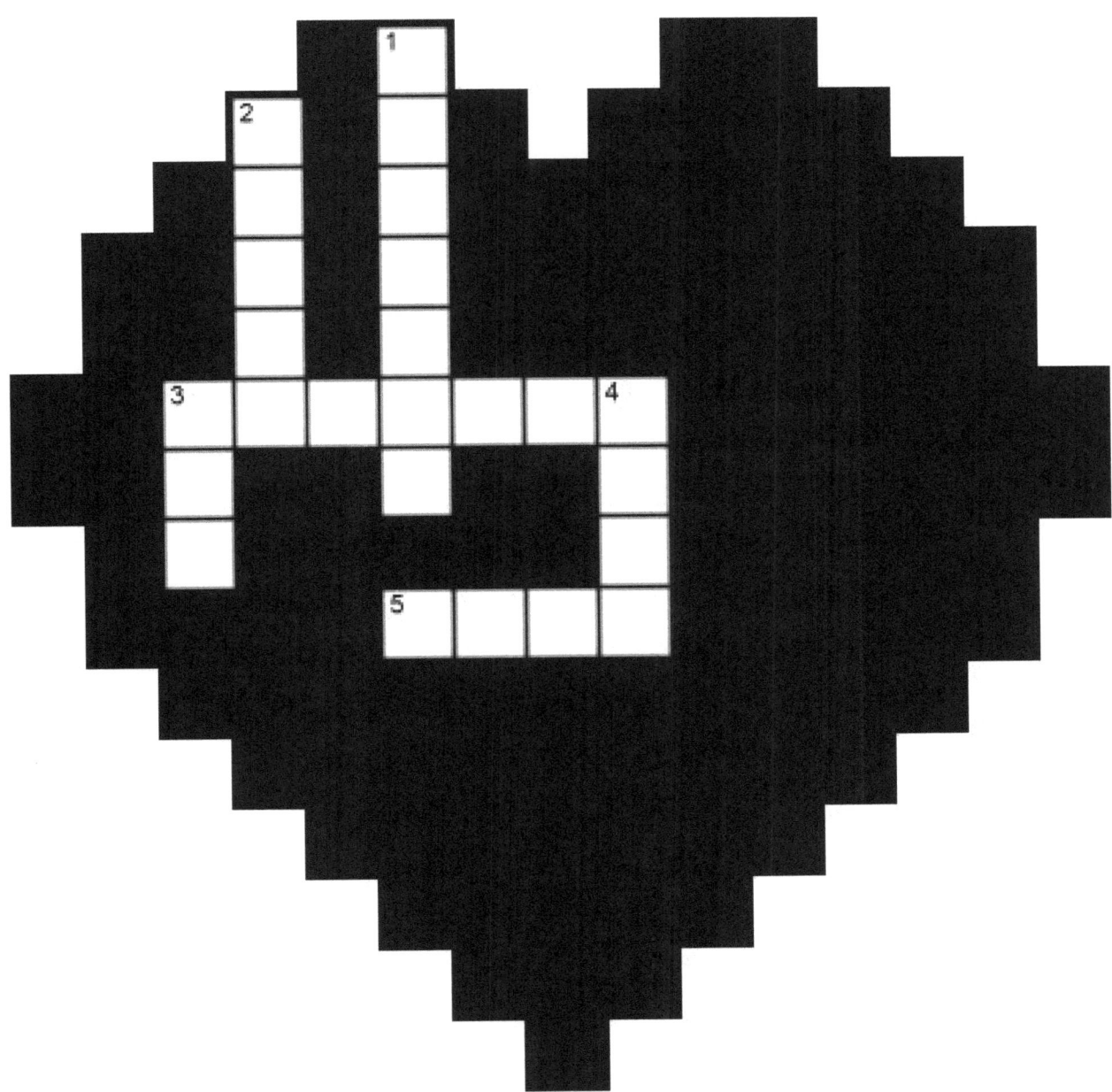

Bravery ~ Daniel 3:8-30

Riddle: We did not obey a law of the king. We were thrown into a firebox. Who are we?

Our Story: We took care of the king's affairs.
But we had to fall down and worship his fake god. We said no.
We were not scared. The king would throw us into his firebox.
We told the king our God would save us. The king's face puffed with rage.
He told his men to add more wood to the firebox.
The fire was seven times hotter. The box shook from the heat.
The king's men put more clothes on us.

Bonus: Name the king.

They threw us into the fire.
The heat from the fire burned the men who threw us in. The king jumped up.
"I see four men not tied. They are walking in the midst of the fire.
They are not hurt. The fourth is like the son of God."
The king called us to come out of the firebox.
Our hair was not burned. We did not smell like smoke.
The king gave praise to our God. The Lord had sent his angel to save us.
We were filled with bravery. Now the king believed in our God.
God blessed us. We did well in the house of the king.

Bravery Clues

Across

3. The king told his men to add more _____ to the firebox. (4)
4. Name the king. (14)

Down

1. The king's men put more _____ on us. (7)
2. We were thrown into a _____ box. (4)
5. The Lord had sent his _____ to save us. (5)
6. The king's face puffed with _____. (4)

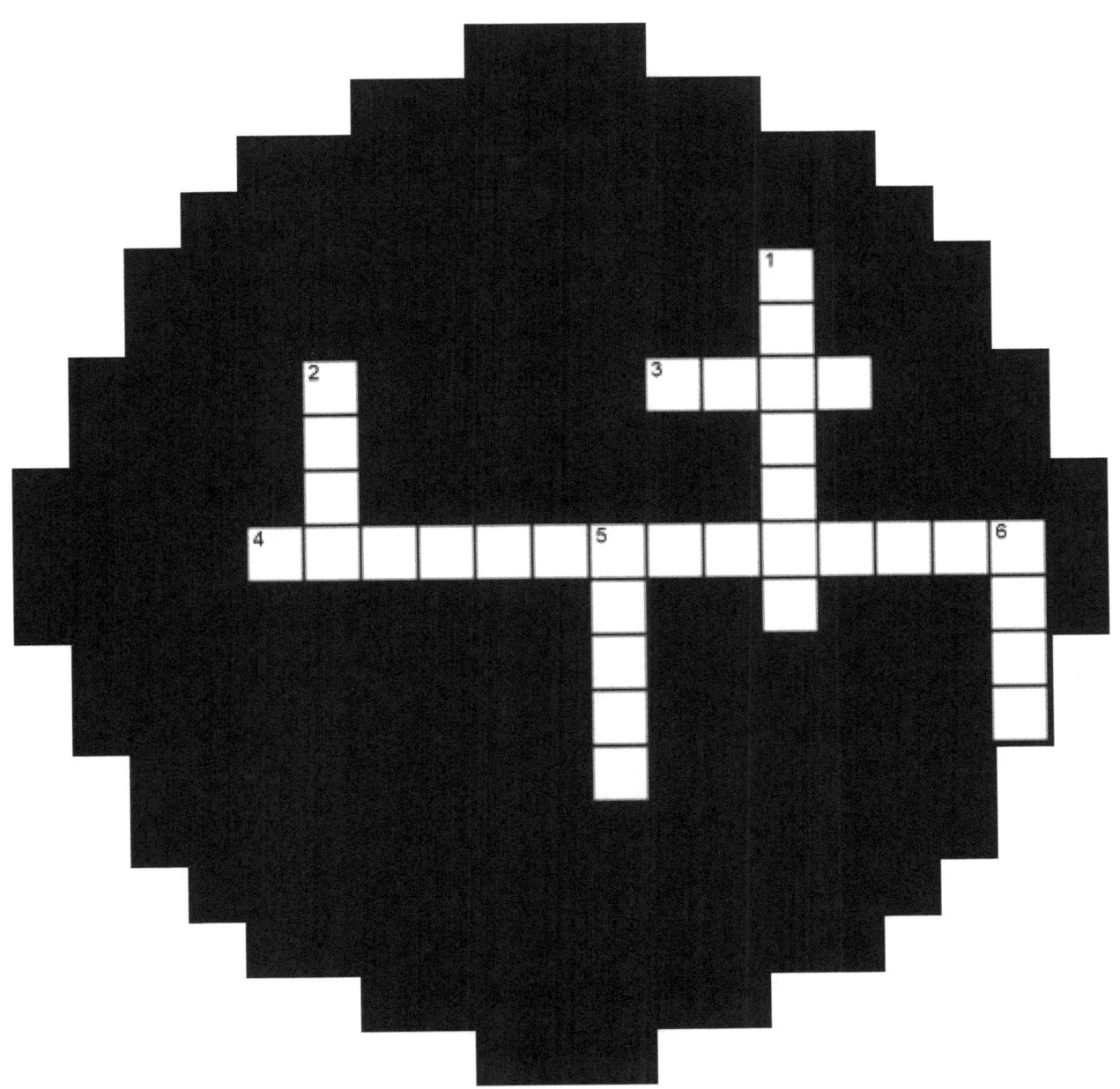

Trustworthy ~ Daniel 6:3-23, 25-28

Riddle: The king who ruled over me was tricked. I almost died. Who am I?

My Story: The king trusted me.
He wanted to make me boss over all the men who ran his kingdom.
The other men did not like that. They tricked the king into making a new law.
People were to pray to the king. Men were to obey the law or die.
I went to my room like I did every day. The upset men watched me.
I did not obey the new law. I prayed to the one true God.
The bad men ran to the king. They told on me.

Trustworthy ~ Daniel 6:3-23, 25-28

Bonus: Name the king.

The king was sad. He did not want to kill me. But he had made the law.
He had to punish me. I had not prayed to him. So, the king put me in a den with the lions.
But the king wanted God to save me. I trusted God in the den of lions.
He would keep me from the jaws of the lions.
The king did not eat or sleep all night. In the day time, the king ran to the den of the lions.
He called to me and asked if God saved me from the lions.
I told him God sent his angel. The angel shut the jaws of the lions.
God saved me as I had trusted in him. And the king believed in God.

Trustworthy Clues

Across

1. I prayed to the one true _____. (3)
3. The other men _____ the king into making a new law. (7)
5. The angel shut the _____ of the lions. (4)
6. The king put me in a den with the _____. (5)

Down

2. Name the king. (6)
4. Who am I? (6)

Puzzle Answers

Creative Being
3. Fowl
4. Adam
5. Eden
1. Feline
2. Peahen

Obedient Builder
2. Creatures
5. Noah
6. Hills
1. Water
3. Sons
4. Glad

Respect of God
2. Isaac
4. Laughter
1. Sarah
3. Cake
5. Abraham
6. Tent

Helpful
5. Rebekah
6. Camels
1. Bracelets
2. Abraham
3. Heart
4. Isaac

Perseverance
3. Brother
5. Father
1. Jacob
2. God
4. Esau
6. Hip

Merciful Brother
1. Brothers
2. Joseph
3. Egypt
1. Bowed
2. Joy
4. Grain

Kinship
2. Slave
3. Freedom
5. Daughter
1. Boat
2. Sister
4. Moses

Spokespersons
1. Two
4. Red
5. Staff
2. Words
3. Snake

Diligence
4. Disobey
5. Angel
1. Money
2. Foes
3. Balaam
4. Donkey

Puzzle Answers

Duty Bound
1. Camp
5. Covenant
6. Jordan
2. Awe
3. Plan
4. Joshua

Kindness
3. Seven
4. Cord
6. Roof
1. Spies
2. Jericho
5. Army

Fairness
1. Sang
3. Deborah
5. Barak
1. Sisera
2. Glory
4. Hear

Valor
2. Gideon
4. Lord
6. Water
1. Angel
3. Trumpets
5. Valor

Spirit-filled Man
2. Strong
4. Lion
1. Judge
2. Samson
3. Rope

Caring Friend
2. Ruth
3. God
5. Boaz
1. Bread
3. Grain
4. Obed

Dependable
3. Vow
5. Dependable
6. Glad
1. Samuel
2. Robe
4. Hannah

Responsible
2. Donkeys
5. Least
6. Heart
1. King
3. Saul
4. Taller

Peacemaker
2. Fear
3. Spirit
5. Oil
1. David
3. Samuel
4. Cow

Puzzle Answers

Courage
1. Bag
4. Giant
5. Five
1. Battle
2. Goliath
3. David

Loyal
2. David
5. Sleep
1. Cave
3. Israel
4. Mean

Wisdom
3. Solomon
4. Gifts
5. Questions
1. Wisdom
2. Songs
3. Sheba

Man of God
2. Samaria
4. Begged
6. Elijah
1. Heaven
3. Angel
5. Captain

Tenacity
4. Elijah
5. Whirlwind
6. Elisha
1. Friend
2. Coat
3. Spirit

Cooperation
3. Mordecai
4. Beg
6. Time
1. Ashes
2. Wrong
5. Esther

Integrity
3. Jemimah
5. Tore
1. Worship
2. Blame
3. Job
4. Hope

Bravery
3. Wood
4. Nebuchadnezzar
1. Clothes
2. Fire
5. Angel
6. Rage

Trustworthy
1. God
3. Tricked
5. Jaws
6. Lions
2. Darius
4. Daniel

Jean Ann Williams lives on the Coast of Oregon with her husband Jim.
She began her writing career in 1994 by reading a stack of books on the craft
of writing. Since then, Jean Ann has published over 300 articles and short stories
on the topics of Christianity, health, travel, friendship, relationships,
family life, Sunday school take-home papers, and the loss of a child by suicide.
This is Jean Ann's eighth book. Her favorite farm animal is the goat.
In her free time, Jean Ann enjoys Crocheting, reading
Inspirational books, gardening, and playing Scrabble with her grandchildren.
Sometimes they let Nana win.

To learn more about Jean Ann Williams visit her on Facebook Author Page:
https://www.facebook.com/Jean-Ann-Williams-848295125269670/Face Book

Carley Herlihy is an artist based in Los Angeles, California.
She started creating book cover designs and illustrations along side
Jean Ann Williams' writing career.
Carley Herlihy has also illustrated other authors' book covers such as
Erik Steins' "No Caution!: A Step-by-Step Guide to
Preparing Auditions for Universities, Colleges, Conservatories, and Beyond."
Carely formatted the book design for "27 Characters of the Old Testament"
and is looking forward to more formatting in the future.

For inquires contact Carley Herlihy at carrosedesigns@gmail.com

Coming in Winter 2024

27 Characters of the New Testament,
Stories & Activities for Children
Matthew through Revelation